30/06/08

To my special lil sis!!
Happy 18th Birthday,
Welcome to the adult world! Hehe!
love you millions,
Jem xxx

What I wish I knew
at eighteen

DANIEL GREGORY & MARTY WILSON

GW00703362

inspired
LIVING

ALLEN&UNWIN

First published in 2008

Copyright © Daniel Gregory and Marty Wilson 2008

Inspired Living, an imprint of
Allen & Unwin
83 Alexander Street
Crows Nest NSW 2065
Australia
Phone: (61 2) 8425 0100
Fax: (61 2) 9906 2218
Email: info@allenandunwin.com
Web: www.allenandunwin.com

National Library of Australia
Cataloguing-in-Publication entry:

   Gregory, Daniel.
   What I wish I knew at eighteen.

   ISBN 978 1 74175 258 8 (pbk.).

   1. Conduct of life - Anecdotes. 2. Spiritual life -
   Anecdotes. I. Wilson, Marty. II. Title.

   158.12

Internal design by Lisa White
Printed in China by Everbest Printing Co., Ltd

10 9 8 7 6 5 4 3 2 1

None of us has all the answers,
but we've all got a few.

If you could go back in time and give your eighteen-year-old self one piece of advice, what would it be?

This is the question we have posed to people of all ages, races, cultures and walks of life.

The answers were extraordinary. Some were funny, others touching and motivating. Every one was filled to the brim with the wisdom of experience.

As we began interviewing people we realised that we are all surrounded by a library of talking books just waiting to be opened up and that each person's advice, though specific to their unique journey through life, has a universal application.

Of course, there were some common themes:

'Be honest with yourself.'

'Do what you love.'

'Take more risks.'

And more than a few said they wouldn't change a thing.

Perhaps the most interesting piece of advice was, 'Make more mistakes'. Mistakes are the events that teach us, give us wisdom and bring about change.

Fortunately, we don't need to make them all ourselves. That is why we decided to write this book.

What I Wish I Knew at Eighteen isn't about regrets or wishing you could go back and change your life; it's about learning from those who have boldly gone before us, inspiring you to think about what you have learned along the way and giving you a gentle push to share that wisdom with those you love.

None of us has all the answers, but here are a few.

Enjoy.

Daniel Gregory & Marty Wilson

The basis of much of our suffering is that we don't understand there are consequences to everything we say and do and think. We want to be victims. We want to find the causes of all our happiness and suffering 'out there' because then we can also dump the blame 'out there'.

Realising that we are the creators of our own experience — the happiness and the suffering — is the beginning of wisdom and the beginning of growing up.

In her twenties, Robina Courtin, 63, was a radical feminist who 'hated half the human race'. In 1976 she attended a Tibetan Buddhist course and was ordained as a Buddhist nun a year later. Robina now works with the Liberation Prison Project, bringing Buddhist teachings to prisoners, including those on death row.

It is possible to be entirely
yourself and still be successful.
You don't have to obscure yourself
through strict conformity.

Being an individual is
what makes you stand out,
what makes you special.

Jim Hunter, 51, spent 25 years in the British army, serving in
Northern Ireland and northern Iraq, and now runs his own business.

Working with Indigenous communities taught me that it doesn't matter how important your work is, or how pressing your deadline; if there's an important event or somebody is sick, you down tools. Life has to be flexible so that the needs of family can come before everything else.

Libby Evans-Illidge, 45, marine biologist, who spent seven years living in the Torres Strait Islands.

Trust yourself.

Know that you know.
You don't have to wait till it feels safe.

Designer Désirée DeKlerk, 50, has learned to approach life with the same courage she brings to facing the terror of the blank page.

Set a goal and fall in love with it so much that you own it, then find a way to afford it.
Don't do it the other way round.

Former accountant Chris Gray, 36, retired from the nine-to-five in his early thirties and now hosts a home TV show.

In 1939 I was separated from my father, declared an enemy of the Soviet Union and packed off on a cattle truck with my mother and her sister to a work camp in Siberia.

I could be miserable about it, but I choose to be grateful.

If it hadn't happened, I wouldn't have met my wife, Madeleine, I wouldn't have my children and grandchildren and I wouldn't have had this wonderful journey.

Look for the good in any bad experience and be grateful.

Polish-born civil engineer Zbigniew Szymanski, 68, survived the Second World War's Siberian work camps and moved to the other side of the world to build a family and a new life.

The thing I've sought my whole
life is the approval of other people,
and that's what's kept me stuck.
Losing that actually sets you free.

Don't wait for the permission
or approval of others:
give it to yourself.

Trish Healy, 33, who got her first taste of freedom as an exchange student in Canada
and now works in human resources helping others fulfil their potential.

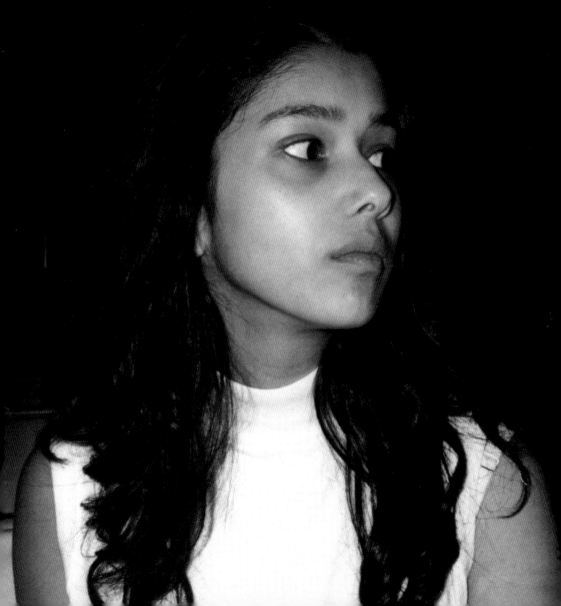

Never intentionally hurt anyone.

Life can be painful, which usually makes us stronger. But those intentional hurts scar us forever. After 9/11, I'll never again intentionally cause another human being pain.

Steve Plakotaris, 49, was in bed with the flu on 11 September 2001 and missed his seat on United Airlines flight 93 which crashed into a field in Pennsylvania, killing all on board.

It's important to have many strings to your bow.
Read everything you can get your hands on.
Be the smartest person in the room.
Make yourself indispensable.

Electrician and production engineer Brian Gregory, 74, left school at
sixteen but never lost his thirst for knowledge.

Stop practising to be a singer and be a singer. Discover the joy of it and let that be enough. Don't practise for so long that you never get around to doing.

At 34, Ana Sevo sings in clubs, at weddings and around the office, having learned that participation is more important than perfection.

I'm a 4'8" woman and not physically strong. For years I felt people could overpower me, that I didn't have the strength to stop people abusing me physically or emotionally, or taking my son away from me. But as I look back on my life, I realise I've been the strong one. Those people saw the strength inside me and wanted it, but didn't know how to get it.

I'd say, 'You have everything you need inside yourself. Mentally, you can get through anything, you can change your life.' That is strength.

Quanita Chivers, 35, mother at fifteen, self-schooled accountant, who was separated from her son for seven years. They are now reunited.

Family isn't just who you're related to; friends can be family too. Family is who you click with, who you can sit with for two hours with nothing said and everything is okay.

Amine Haddad, 48, a family man who now manages a company started by a friend he met at university.

I remember sitting with my seven-year-old daughter in the hospital while she was having eight big vials of blood taken and she was laughing. The doctor said, 'Don't laugh, you'll hurt yourself.'

Afterwards my daughter told me, 'Mummy, if I didn't laugh, I'd cry.'

A sense of humour gets you through a lot.

Anne Robinson, 63, a mother of three, nursed one daughter through a back operation and another through a kidney transplant.

Intolerance is learned.

No child starts out hating Russians or communists or Aborigines.

Former school principal Stewart John (Mac) McCoullough, OAM, 80, earned the love of his students and the respect of his community.

If you're not true to yourself, you just end up coming back and doing what's true later. You can't run from yourself forever.

Paul Alexandrou, 33, a film director and non-practising lawyer now working as a writer in London.

I remember hating food until I was twenty — it was purely functional and tied to poor body image. It was a revelation to discover that taking the trouble to cook for people, to learn how to make a new meal and to then share it, is a universal and delightful expression of love. Food is not just something practical you have to attend to three times a day. It's a wonderful way of sharing life.

Lucy Faulkner, 36, wine buyer, music teacher, food lover.

Stumble a lot and often. Make mistakes.

Do things that you might regret so you can build up a vocabulary of life experiences. Only then will the decisions you make about how to live be meaningful to you as opposed to simply adopting conventional ways of behaving. Having made so many mistakes in my life I've developed a lot more compassion for other people's errors, foibles and weaknesses.

David Thompson, 42, is a world-renowned chef who fell in love with Thailand's people, culture and food.

Know, just know with absolute certainty that you have an inner guidance, an inner voice, a vision that is calling you and bringing out a mission in you that is not something small.

It is very profound.

Dr John Demartini, 52, almost died of severe strychnine poisoning as a seventeen-year-old before finding his life's purpose as an inspirational writer and speaker.

People are a mirror of you.
If a person upsets you it is because you are seeing something in yourself that you dislike.

Born of Chinese parents in Malaysia, Arnyi Tan, 61, is a Qigong practitioner living in Australia who balances the yin and yang of being both Asian and western.

Mark Kelly, 50, is a
magazine publisher
who'd rather be
in Canada skiing.

You are only accountable to yourself.

Make yourself proud and that's enough.

(Oh! And your mother.)

People I never gave a chance at university turned out to be great people.

So I'd say to myself at eighteen, 'Don't just stick to your own friends. Make an effort to talk to people who don't fit the usual mould — they can challenge your thinking and make life much more interesting.'

Don't hit 50 and still have only the same friends you had in high school.

A farmer's son, John Madden, 36, travelled the world working as an agricultural economist and appreciates the importance of diversity.

Three days a week I'd stick two 15-gauge needles into my left arm and watch my blood pump through a filter for hours on end.

Then, after six years on a transplant waiting list, I got the call to say a kidney was on its way to the hospital for me. That amazing gift from someone I'd never met changed my life forever.

All of a sudden, I had freedom. I could do anything. There was nothing to hold me back.

What would I tell my eighteen-year-old self today?

You need to enjoy every minute. Definitely, definitely, don't put off till tomorrow what you can enjoy today.

Debbie Cheng, 34, whose kidney transplant gave her the future she dreamed of. Now a wife to Geoff and mother to Liam.

Seek balance.

You need it in cooking for flavour,
and you need it in life.
You need those times when you're working
intensely and you need those times with your
family enjoying good food and great wine.

Neil Perry, 45, chef, restaurant owner, cookbook author, television presenter.

Having the latest clothes or a great haircut doesn't matter. It's how you carry yourself, what you believe in and who you are that make you attractive.

After her parents split when she was sixteen, Nickie Powell, now 35, spent many years working out her own definition of love. She married her long-time boyfriend in 2003.

Be more tolerant.

Not everything is black and white.

A retired teacher and mother of two daughters, Mega Moodley, 63, grew up in South Africa under apartheid as a 'non-white'.

I've had too many friends commit suicide, people who have all contributed immensely to my life. I can't judge them because they must have been terribly lost and lonely but I do wonder whether I took enough time to extend the hand of friendship to them. So I'd say to the eighteen-year-old me to never, ever let the opportunity pass to tell your friends how much they mean to you.

When Matt Laffan was born with a rare genetic disorder his parents were told he wouldn't survive. Thirty-eight years later he is a distinguished lawyer and a tireless charity worker.

No one religion is right.

There are so many ingrained truths that are common to all faiths that you have to stay open and accepting. It's ridiculous to think people kill each other based on which church they go to on the weekend to pray to the same god.

Denise Douglas, 34, is a Northern Irish Protestant who had only met one Catholic before she went to university.

Do not have goals — they're too limiting! My career has taught me that things work out much better than I would ever have been audacious enough to ask or pray for.

Just do what you love and see what unfolds.

Ken Roberts, 56, is a commodity trader and cigar connoisseur who helps people all around the world build their own businesses.

It comes down to something simple like a shared sense of humour, being able to have fun when it's just the two of you.

Laughter is incredibly important.

Christine and Ian Witter, 59 and 60, met in their teens, married in their twenties, made a home for three daughters and a son (and a hungry horde of cousins and friends), and are still laughing together 35 years later.

Ninety-eight per cent of what you fear, obsess about and have panic attacks over never, ever happens.

With a Sicilian mother, a father from Sierra Leone and a British upbringing, Chantal Badjie, 47, counts figuring out who she is as one of her greatest achievements.

Don't be a health freak, be an athlete.

An athlete is someone who studies the mechanics of the body and gets it to work correctly. A health freak is someone who pushes their body till it snaps.

Chris Neill, 56, is an athlete, martial artist, kinesiologist and body mechanic.

Doing things that challenge you transforms the way you see your life. It keeps your expectations growing. It's only afterwards that you say: 'I knew I could do it.'

The more you do, the more you can imagine doing.

Hetty Read, 32, communications manager at the BBC, marathon runner and columnist for the *Jersey Evening Post*.

When you're young you treat older people differently because they look different to you. As you get older you realise that, inside at least, you feel the same as you did when you were in your twenties. No one feels like an 'old person' — on the inside everyone is just 'a person'.

Donna Wilson, 61, left school at fifteen to become a radio music programmer and a dental nurse. She is now a grandmother of nine.

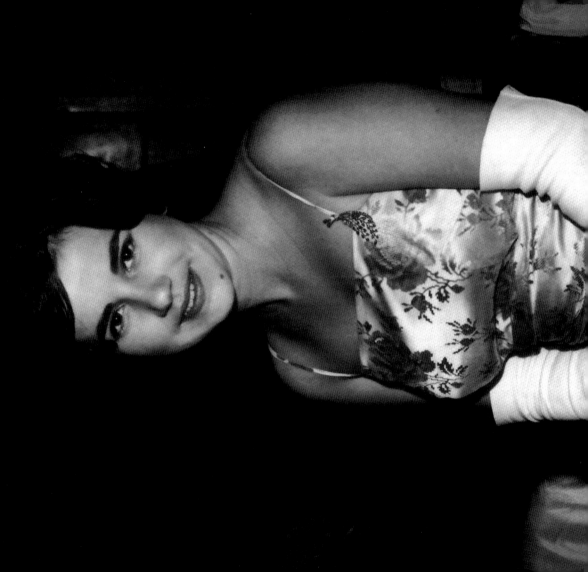

Once you get to know the people you're told to hate, you realise they're no different to you.

Nigel Miller, 35, a Catholic from Omagh, Northern Ireland, arrived home from a year of travelling on the day the Real IRA bombed the town centre.

There's an invisible box around each of us. People like to keep you locked inside: you're allowed to go to the edges, just not outside. 'Please don't be more than us.'

There's a world outside to be explored, so jump out of the box.

Kieran Flanagan, 35, creative director, who has a passion for interior design and her Staffordshire terrier puppy, Stella.

Nobody owns the truth.

The minute you start travelling you
discover words, opinions and concepts
in other languages that don't even exist
in your own.
Be a traveller, not a tourist.
Eat the weird food.
Drink the strange coffee.
Go into the dodgy bar.

Karl Dunn, 36, a traveller who still calls Ontario,
Manitoba, Sydney, Singapore, Berlin, Tokyo, Amsterdam,
Johannesburg and Los Angeles home.

When I was eighteen, I was training very hard and fortunately it developed into a habit that kept me feeling young all my life. I only stopped running 5 miles a day, as fast as in my playing days, at age 75. I don't regret one of the hundreds of miles I ran. They gave me the pleasure of being able to do things at 45 that other blokes had to stop doing at 35. If you're interested in sport or just interested in life, work on your fitness.

You can't fully enjoy life unless you're healthy.

Trevor Allan, Wallaby captain for three years, rugby commentator for 27, lover of life for 80. (Sadly, Trevor passed away before this book was finished.)

When you're young you think your success is all your own doing. As you get older you realise how many people it takes to make even the simplest venture come together, and you appreciate everyone who has helped you get where you are.

Thank more people, more often.

Mathew Dickerson, 39, award-winning businessman and deputy mayor, on the myth of being a 'self-made man'.

Make your future bigger
than your past by
seeking growth rather
than applause.

**Siimon Reynolds, 43, advertising guru, bestselling author
and passionate student of human achievement.**

Having kids is instantly transformative. You suddenly realise you are part of a chain of events — when you're young you think you are the event.

Craig Davis, 41, son, husband, and father of three.

After I was diagnosed with breast cancer I found myself experiencing my days through the eyes of death and, in the process, began to marvel at life. I imagined what I would savour if I were re-living each moment from my deathbed. I began to see and feel things that usually passed me by — the beauty of light in the trees, the miraculous sound of my child gently breathing and the smell of spring in the air. So I'd say to my younger self: 'Try not to get lost in the past or future, they don't really exist. The pasture is greenest right here, right now.'

Meredith Hope, 36, breast cancer survivor, who had her first course of chemotherapy just two weeks before her wedding.

I work in a world of elitism and achievement. Having two kids with disabilities gave me an appreciation of things that I would never otherwise have got: perseverance, tolerance, patience. My kids have taught me that life's about doing your best, no matter whether you're playing for your national team, running around in C-Grade or just trying to live through another day.

Father of three, former police officer, international rugby league player and coach Wayne Bennett, 58.

Most people confuse fame with talent.

Fifty years ago people who achieved worthwhile goals sometimes became well known. Now people see fame itself as the goal. I'd rather be unknown than be famous for something that is meaningless and worthless.

Artie Laing, 42, grew up watching his father tour leading bands. He is now an entertainment agent.

The more you plan your future, the more you become predictable and the greater danger you are in.

Glynn Braddy, 65, an architect and philosopher who has spent his life improving the health of others and learned to heal himself after a stroke.

Stop eating, unless it's humble pie. Humility is the only weight worth carrying around with you through the years.

Karen Wong, 34, a businesswoman who travels around the world with her career and watches her mental diet.

Find those areas in life that make you uncomfortable, that make your palms sweat. That's where the growth is.

Matt Sherring, 45, who bit the bullet and moved to New York.
He and a friend have since sold their first screenplay.

1. Don't worry about what people think of you; everyone is way too busy thinking about themselves.

2. No one has a clue what they are doing — some people are just better at looking like they do.

3. Always have champagne chilling in the fridge. It looks sophisticated and encourages impromptu celebrations.

Rachel Donath, 30, new business consultant and scuba enthusiast on looking and feeling your best.

Learn to appreciate what you do.

I was filming at NASA, surrounded by astronauts, and I started talking to a mission controller for the Apollo missions. He kept asking questions about my career as a cameraman. This guy put a man on the moon and he's interested in what I do!

Emmy-winning cameraman and pilot Mark Walker, 38, has covered stories as varied as Hollywood's A-list parties and the attacks on the Twin Towers on 9/11.

In your person-to-person dealings, honour your word and do business by the shake of a hand.

Eric McGraw, 82, who grew up in a boys' home and went on to own a hardware store, a pool maintenance company, and an electrical contracting business he has now passed on to his son.

The passive approach doesn't always work. Sometimes you need to assert yourself, not sit back timidly.

You need to command respect.

Bruce Gregory, 36, a quiet, talented artist and musician, and a police officer.

When you have an argument with your partner — and you will — never go to sleep without saying sorry. You can disagree all evening, sometimes even all day, but always make up before you turn off the light.

Separated for five years from her new husband, Len, by the Second World War, Betty Salter went on to be happily married for 54 of her 86 years.

I'd say to my eighteen-year-old self:
'Okay, so you're sad, angry, intense, hopeless
and pessimistic now. You don't know this
yet but there is something inside you that is
good, that is special. If you give it a chance,
that unique spark can grow and flourish.'

Give life a little bit of time and I promise something good will come of it.

Ant Melder, 35, left school at sixteen and ran a magazine called
No Future. He went travelling, found some answers and now has
a family and a career as a published author.

When I was growing up my relationship with my dad was practically nonexistent so I always went for men who made me fight for their love.

The wonderful man I ended up with is the polar opposite of everyone I had ever dated: stable, calm and generous.

So I'd say to myself at eighteen: 'Don't go for the gorgeous guy standing on the pool table shouting, "I am a god. Worship me!" Give the not-quite-so-exciting, slightly badly dressed man standing in the corner a chance. Go talk to him and you'll end up incredibly happy and fulfilled.'

Tanja Bernhardt, 36, on finding a 'perfect' partner.

So many people seem to be in a perpetual state of misery over what they don't like about their lives.

You don't get happy, acquire happy or achieve happy; you just decide to be happy.

After surviving a horrific motorcycle accident Simon MacRae, 36, began writing with his brother, Kenn. They have just released their first feature film, *The View from Greenhaven*.

Don't be afraid to try different things to work out
what you want to do in life, even if others may not
understand. You're a long time working — if you don't
love your job it'll break you.

Kieren Callaghan, 40, trader (and former chef, former trainee mechanic, former
home security door-to-door salesman, former tractor spray-painter . . .).

Never ask a question unless you can:
a. handle the answer
b. understand the consequences.

Bill Healy, 63, drummer, travel agent, teacher, writer,
broadcaster, Roy Orbison fan and TV travel-show presenter.

The crucial thing I wish I had known at eighteen, or 28, is that my life is precious.

I certainly valued 'life' and other people's lives. But self-acceptance was a foreign idea and self-love was off the radar. I confused it with self-absorption and thought the best way to make myself a 'better person' was to be relentlessly self-critical. My mother had died when I was eight so I missed seeing myself through her loving and accepting eyes.

At eighteen I was ambitious to do something worthwhile, but doubted I was worthwhile myself. I routinely took risks. I sometimes felt devastatingly lonely. From those times, I learned compassion. But I learned it slowly. And I learned to apply it to myself last of all. It takes courage to value our lives not so much for what we can do with them but for the priceless gift that each of them is.

Stephanie Dowrick, 61, author, psychotherapist, mother of two and ordained interfaith minister.

In my wallet I keep a page I clipped out of a long-forgotten magazine which shows how all major religions have a common belief in what has become known as 'The Golden Rule':

Christianity: 'So in everything, do to others what you would have them do to you, for this sums up the Law and all the Prophets.' Matthew 7:12

Buddhism: 'Hurt not others in ways that you yourself would find hurtful.' Udana-Varga 5.18

Judaism: 'What is hateful to you, do not do to your fellow man. That is the entire law: all the rest is commentary.' The Talmud, Shabbat 31a

Islam: 'No one of you truly believes until he desires for his brother that which he desires for himself.' Number 13 of Al-Nawawi's Forty Hadiths

Hinduism: 'This is the sum of duty; do nothing to others, which, if done to you, would cause you pain.' The Mahabharata 5, 1517

Paul Wilson, 65, a pharmacist, on the world's best medicine.

Pay attention to the questions you ask yourself, because if you improve the quality of those questions you lift the quality of your life.

Life coach Anni Haque, 49, defines her own success by what she brings out in others.

Your health and wellbeing has to be a priority.

We all want success, we all want the pats on the back and we all want money in the bank but it's all meaningless if you don't have the ability to enjoy it.

Ian Robson, 44, CEO of Hawthorn Football Club, says he feels most successful when his kids run down the hall to him when he gets home.

You're not too fat,
you're not too thin,
you're not too tall,
you're not too short,
your boobs aren't too big,
your boobs aren't too small,
your bum isn't too big,
you don't have the wrong type of hair
and your hair is not the wrong colour.

After twenty years' nursing and having seen both the great and the lowly
stark naked, Laura Robertson, 41, knows a thing or two about body image.

Human beings are inherently kind.

You have nothing to fear from anyone whose culture, belief systems and tastes differ from your own.

On becoming an artist and author, ex-paratroop platoon commander Bradley Trevor Greive, 37, discovered the pen was indeed mightier than the M16 assault rifle.

When people tell me they hate their job I feel like saying, 'What! You think you're going to live forever?' Why work at something you despise? If you're not doing something you love you're missing the whole point of life. Soon you'll be 88 years old and thinking: 'Didn't I turn eighteen a few days ago?'

Born in a small country town, Christina Leonard, 35, went on to study at Sydney's Conservatorium of Music and now plays with the Sydney Symphony and Australian Opera and Ballet Orchestras.

Never let the fear of losing your house, car
or job dictate who you are.
When you breathe your last, and give those
daisies the death grip, the only thing that
matters is whether you lived your life by
your own rules, or someone else's.

Former teen mother Tammy Romer, 43, is a reiki practitioner
and works in an infant education company in Portland, Oregon.

Think about how what
you're doing is going to
cost you in the future.
Everything in life has a
price tag.

Ex-hairdresser, ex-dancer and
salesman Gary Fishburn, 48,
decided to take life's scenic route.

I decided to make money at what I was good at and leave what I loved for my spare time. There is no spare time.

There is no spare time.

Harvard graduate and managing director Steven Johnston, 49, enjoys playing the drums in his 'spare time'.

Don't procrastinate, don't hesitate.

There's the gap, take it.
There's the job, ask for it.
There's the girl, ask her out. If you say, 'I'll ask her out next week', by next week she'll have a boyfriend.

Stand-up comic and actor Anh Do, 30, left Vietnam with his family on an 8-metre fishing boat. They were shot at by communists, attacked by pirates, and ran out of food and water two days before a German merchant ship found them.

All my life I thought I'd go back to Sri Lanka and everyone would be just like me. When I got there and the nun said, 'We know where your mother is. We can have you there in ten minutes', I realised that I already had the mother I was searching for.

The love you go looking for is at home waiting for you.

Matt Forrester, 25, who was adopted in Sri Lanka and raised in Australia, on learning the true meaning of family.

Yelling and screaming at people is never the answer. Be considerate to those you employ. Show them they're part of a team. Show them they're important. Show them they're valued.

Factory manager and business owner Graham Robinson, 66, retired to show his three daughters and their children just how valuable they are to him.

Money is great but it's not worth
sacrificing everything for.
Some of the richest people you
meet are some of the poorest.

While Peter Fallon, 39, spends his days valuing real estate, his wife and children have
taught him to appreciate the things in life that are priceless.

Don't at any point entertain the idea
that you have to be like somebody
else in order to succeed.
Don't run away from what you've
experienced or try to change yourself.

Just tell the truth.

The more truthful you are, the bigger
the laugh, the larger the response, the
better the show, the longer the season.

Actor and comic Mary Coustas, 42, found fame
by being true to her Greek heritage.

You'd be surprised at how tough you are. You don't realise what you can get through if you have to.

Andrew Hampson, 40, ran marathons and competed in triathlons until, at 22, a rugby injury confined him to a wheelchair for life. He works as a statistical analyst and recently bought his own apartment.

Our internal dialogue can be vicious and outrageous. If someone spoke to us the way we speak to ourselves we would never talk to them again. Have compassion for yourself, especially in the tough times.

Give yourself the same love and kindness that you show others.

After ten years of acting, performing her one-woman play for Kenneth Branagh's Renaissance Theatre Company, Lucy Ratcliffe, 40, is now coaching others to perform in business.

Don't try to win more than 30 per cent of the arguments. A happy wife is a happy life.

Arthur Tonkiss, 80, is a very happily married man, who gets it right 80 per cent of the time, but is smart enough to keep this to himself.

Don't be a frustrated anything.

Andy Healy, 35, frustrated lyricist,
frustrated drummer, frustrated guitarist.

Find what you love and practise it. Daily.

Then one day, years later, people will forget all the hard work and call you talented.

Award-winning cellist and pianist, now music teacher, Lillah Gregory, 67, believes talent is as much earned as it is inherited.

Working in an emergency unit
makes you realise that the quality
of life can change abruptly and
that life itself can end instantly. So
for me, success in life has nothing
to do with wealth or material
possessions. It's having the guts to
try things — travel, singing lessons,
korfball, acting classes, whatever.
Even if it doesn't pan out, I tried.

For me, success is the trying.

Neil Fletcher, 37, runs a paediatric emergency unit and was
last seen heading to Spain for a netball tournament.

Life is too precious
to waste time worrying.

In 1943 George Blakeman was shot down over France but survived, thanks to his parachute which was blown open by the explosion. At 85, he parachuted out of a plane to raise money for research into Alzheimer's disease, which claimed his wife of 57 years.

Be brave.

In those tiny moments of choice, when you stay
fearless instead of being sensible and rational,
it always works out better.

Without any training in film-making, Matt Duffy, 38, a former lawyer and first-grade
rugby player, took the plunge and now makes his own documentaries.

Appreciate what you've got now
and stop looking for what you
might have in the future.

Midwife Liane Powell, 35, wrote goodbye letters to her husband and children before
successful surgery to remove a brain tumour. She now takes nothing for granted.

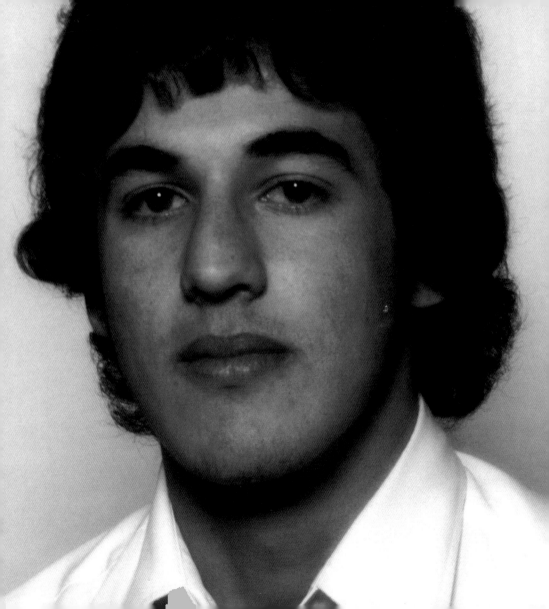

Accept that every courageous decision, especially those which take you closer to some dream, comes with a consequence. There's always a price to pay.

Be willing to let go of the things that don't matter so much.

Father, entrepreneur and businessman George Betsis, 48, spends his week building companies with a nurturing culture and the weekend watching his son play soccer.

The particular path I found myself taking in life, while not what I intended, led me to meet my husband and to have two beautiful children. I wouldn't give that up for anything.

If I had the opportunity to go back in time and change things, I wouldn't.

Simone Carton, 33, founder of three film festivals, discovered that not sticking to 'the plan' is sometimes part of the plan.

Learn from history
and pass your own
knowledge on.

Retired sales manager John Hulme, 73, who grew up as an only child
while his older brothers were away at war, knows the value of listening
to those who've gone before.

If you take the time to
really listen, almost everyone
you meet can give you
something incredibly valuable.

No matter what you're trying to achieve or work through, there's usually someone within your extended circle of friends and family who can offer some useful advice. And if you don't already know someone who can help, find someone who can. People who are passionate about living well are always open to sharing the benefit of their experience.

Want to be a better mother or father? Call up every great parent you know and ask them for some tips. Want to be a writer? Sidle up to a published author at a party and offer to buy them dinner if they'll share some secrets about their work. We did just that, and now we're published authors. Want to be a better partner, leader, accountant, singer, anything? Take a good look around. You're surrounded by people who can help you learn and evolve more quickly.

Cast your net far and wide. We discovered that when you reach out and talk about life's really big issues, you not only get some great advice but you also make some wonderful new friends and discover a whole different side to those you've known for years.

Enjoy the journey,

Daniel & Marty

[photo here]

Name: ....

What do you wish you knew at eighteen?

....

....

....

....

....

....

....

....

....

....

ACKNOWLEDGMENTS

Daniel and Marty would like to thank all the extraordinary people who gave their time and shared their wisdom so generously. You made this book possible. Particular thanks go to Bradley Greive for taking the time to say, 'Hey, I'm writing a book, you should too'. They'd also like to acknowledge Mathew Alderson, their lawyer extraordinaire, and of course, a big thank you to Maggie Hamilton, Clara Finlay, Lisa White and the brilliant team at Allen & Unwin for their limitless enthusiasm and encouragement. Daniel would also like to thank his inspirational wife Kerryanne for her amazing capacity to believe in him, his dearest friends Kieran, George and Andy for keeping him sane, his loving family for their support, and of course Marty, for sharing this 10-year journey. Marty wants to thank Danny G for sharing his ideas and his ruthless energy, his family for supporting his 'brilliant career', his boys, Connor and Elliot, for giving him a reason, and his amazing wife, Allie, whose tenderness and patience leave him in awe.

PS We want to share the gift of hindsight by publishing more books in the *What I Wish I Knew at Eighteen* series and would love to hear from anyone who has learned from experience about life, love and success. If you know someone extraordinary, someone whose insights would be a gift to the world, please contact us at **www.whatiwishiknew.com**.